Over Two and a Half Hours of Video Instruction!

# Nashville HOT PICKIN' GUITAR
## by Matthew Lee

## Contents

Introduction . . . . . . . . . . . . . . . . . . . . . . 2

Basic Concepts . . . . . . . . . . . . . . . . . . . 3

Scales . . . . . . . . . . . . . . . . . . . . . . . 10

The CAGED System . . . . . . . . . . . . . . 17

Country Techniques. . . . . . . . . . . . . . 22

Putting the Pieces Together . . . . . . . 37

Recommended Guitar Players . . . . . 48

About the Author. . . . . . . . . . . . . . . . 48

To access video visit:
**www.halleonard.com/mylibrary**

Enter Code
1514-9002-8530-7163

ISBN 978-1-5400-7285-0

**HAL•LEONARD®**

Visit Hal Leonard Online at
**www.halleonard.com**

Contact us:
**Hal Leonard**
7777 West Bluemound Road
Milwaukee, WI 53213
Email: info@halleonard.com

In Europe, contact:
**Hal Leonard Europe Limited**
42 Wigmore Street
Marylebone, London, W1U 2RN
Email: info@halleonardeurope.com

In Australia, contact:
**Hal Leonard Australia Pty. Ltd.**
4 Lentara Court
Cheltenham, Victoria, 3192 Australia
Email: info@halleonard.com.au

# Introduction ▶

As you begin to dive into this book, my hope is that upon completion you have a much better understanding of what encompasses great country guitar playing. I've spent over a decade in Nashville gathering styles, licks, techniques, and ways I believe are best to produce a professional-sounding music product. In this book, I will show you the lessons I've learned and how to get the most out of your playing. I will cover concepts from basic to advanced that span a wide range of topics in the honky-tonk guitar style. These concepts are important to know to become not only a better guitar player but a great musician, as well.

Country guitar playing and specifically, hybrid picking, is a delicate dance between the right and left hands. Coordination and execution between both hands is a must in order to properly play the ideas and techniques shown in this book. Start slow and work your way up in tempo to consistently play the lines shown. There are several examples for each topic discussed, and these examples start relatively easy and move to more difficult and advanced playing. Work at your own pace, set goals, and try to achieve them when moving through each lesson in the book. It should be assumed that you possess a basic understanding of music theory and the ability to recognize note names and chord symbols, so tablature and standard notation have been provided to help in the learning process. Each example is demonstrated with accompanying videos which can be accessed by going to *www.halleonard.com/mylibrary* and inputting the code found on page 1 of this book.

Remember that you are working just as much on the mental comprehension as you are the physical understanding of playing guitar with this book. Be cognizant of the note selection over each chord, especially articulations (slides, slurs, etc.), and use this information to inspire yourself to create a whole new database of licks and tricks in your own style. I appreciate you choosing this book, and I look forward to being your guide on this honky-tonk journey. Let's get started!

# Basic Concepts

## Hybrid Picking

The preferred right-hand technique of most country guitar players is called **hybrid picking**. This is a combination of using a pick with your thumb and index finger to play the bass strings while using the middle and ring fingers on the right hand to pluck higher-pitched strings. This allows you to get the "snap," "pop," or "cluck" sound when striking notes. To properly use this technique, you will need to have independence with your pick (indicated with "p") while also using the middle ("m") and ring ("a") fingers on the right hand. Example 1 is a great way to get comfortable using this technique. Let the notes ring out and use a cascading motion in the right hand, playing the pick first, then the middle and ring fingers, respectively. The pattern is a triplet pattern, or grouping in three.

**Example 1**

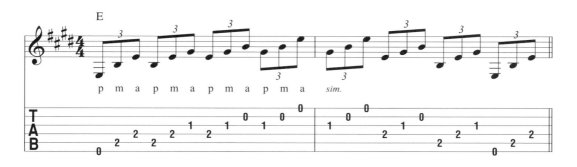

Example 2 takes you through a basic chord progression while focusing on this technique. Make sure to let the notes ring out and play the rhythm in groupings of three. Your wrist should be relatively flat while resting your palm on the bridge of the guitar, gliding up or down as dictated by the pattern.

**Example 2** 2:00

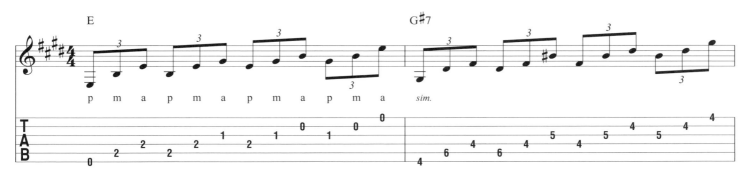

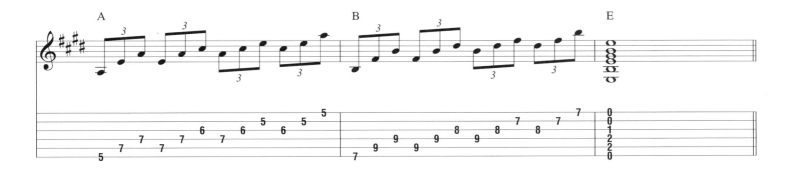

Example 3 is a very common rhythm used in country music over an A chord. In this example, each string is covered by a pick, middle, or ring finger. The pick stays on the A string (you can play it muted, as shown in the video) while the middle finger is on the D string and the ring finger is on the G. The middle and ring fingers work together, playing two notes at once and with hammer-ons/pull-offs. This example is a great way to practice right-hand independence while throwing in some other articulations.

**Example 3**  3:12

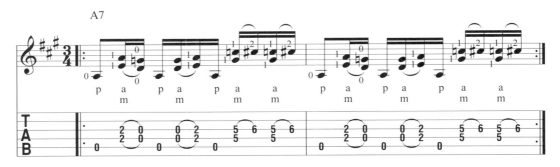

Example 4 is a classic way of comping over an E chord. Also included at the end of the bar is a single-note fill. The last note in this bar should be played with your middle finger on your right hand—try to snap the note in an upward motion. This will give you that authentic "country" sound. Make sure to use proper right-hand technique similar to Example 3 and be able to play both examples over and over. I highly recommend playing these with a metronome or drum beat. Start slow, and work your way up in tempo.

**Example 4**  4:33

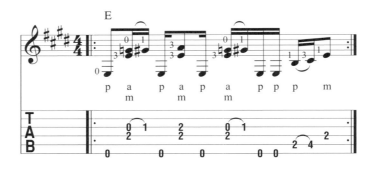

# Knowing the Neck

Getting to know the guitar neck and which notes you are playing is crucial to understanding what you're playing, interacting with other musicians, and learning at a quicker pace. On the next page are the ABCs of all music on all instruments: the **chromatic scale**. These 12 notes are the building blocks for all music, and it is essential to know how they're related and where they are located on the guitar neck. Below is the chromatic scale and where all notes are located on the guitar neck. Get to know the neck intimately. This is essential to understanding not only what other players are doing with note choices but also your preferences regarding certain situations. You will also be able to communicate more easily with musicians and have a deeper understanding of patterns and sequences over chord progressions as a soloist, not just the fret numbers you're playing.

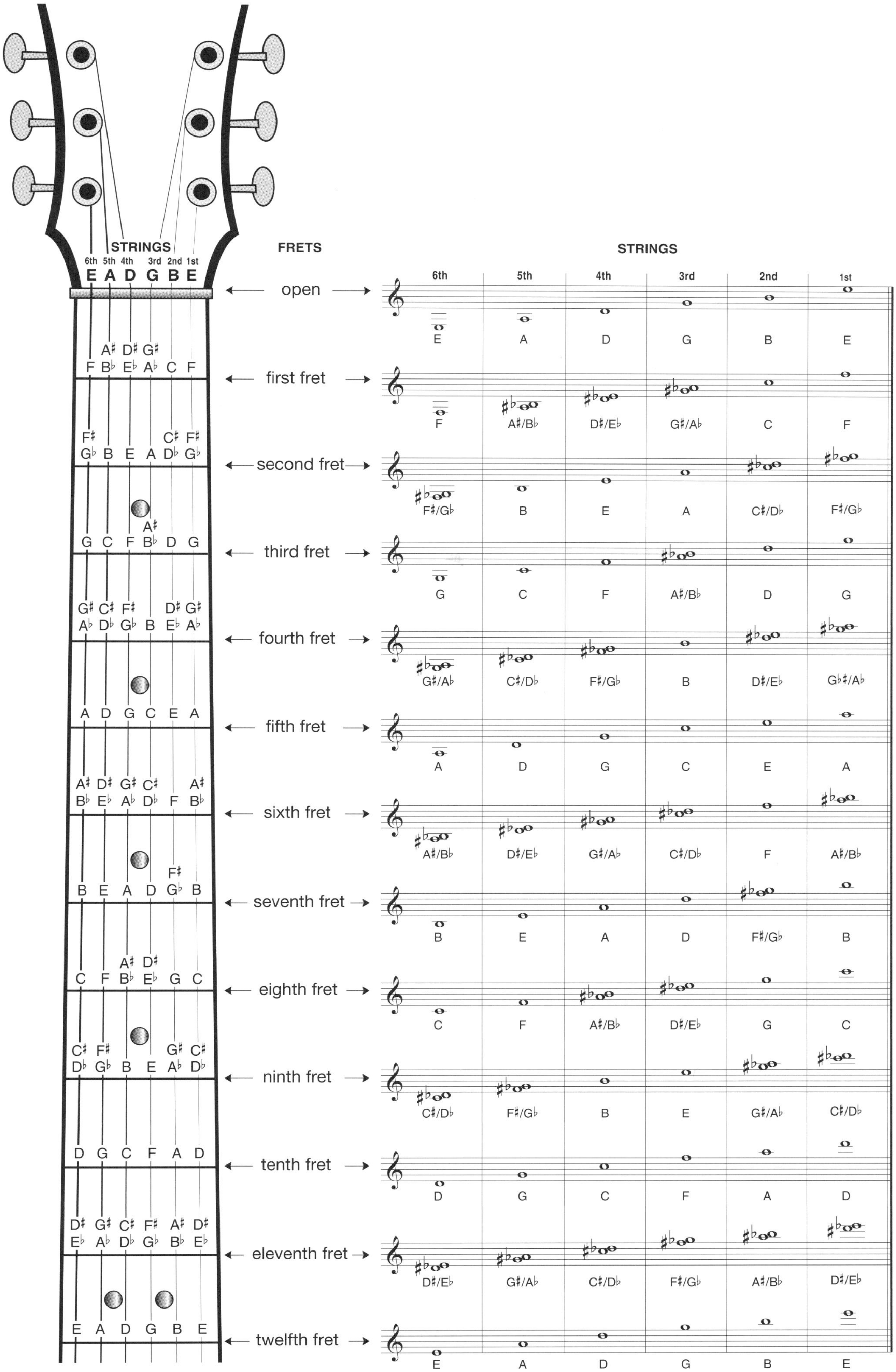

STRINGS     FRETS     STRINGS

6th 5th 4th 3rd 2nd 1st

**E A D G B E**

| | 6th | 5th | 4th | 3rd | 2nd | 1st |
|---|---|---|---|---|---|---|
| **open** | E | A | D | G | B | E |
| **first fret** | F | A#/Bb | D#/Eb | G#/Ab | C | F |
| **second fret** | F#/Gb | B | E | A | C#/Db | F#/Gb |
| **third fret** | G | C | F | A#/Bb | D | G |
| **fourth fret** | G#/Ab | C#/Db | F#/Gb | B | D#/Eb | Gb#/Ab |
| **fifth fret** | A | D | G | C | E | A |
| **sixth fret** | A#/Bb | D#/Eb | G#/Ab | C#/Db | F | A#/Bb |
| **seventh fret** | B | E | A | D | F#/Gb | B |
| **eighth fret** | C | F | A#/Bb | D#/Eb | G | C |
| **ninth fret** | C#/Db | F#/Gb | B | E | G#/Ab | C#/Db |
| **tenth fret** | D | G | C | F | A | D |
| **eleventh fret** | D#/Eb | G#/Ab | C#/Db | F#/Gb | A#/Bb | D#/Eb |
| **twelfth fret** | E | A | D | G | B | E |

Fretboard note names (left diagram):

first fret: A# F | D# Bb | G# Eb | Ab(A#) | C | F
(F Bb Eb Ab C F)

second fret: F# G# | B | E | A | C# Db | F# Gb
(G# B E A Db G#)

third fret: G C F Bb (A#) D G

fourth fret: G# Ab | C# Db | F# Gb | B | D# Eb | G# Ab

fifth fret: A D G C E A

sixth fret: A# Bb | D# Eb | G# Ab | C# Db | F | A# Bb

seventh fret: B E A D F# Gb B

eighth fret: C F A# Bb | D# Eb | G C

ninth fret: C# Db | F# Gb | B E | G# Ab | C# Db

tenth fret: D G C F A D

eleventh fret: D# Eb | G# Ab | C# Db | F# Gb | A# Bb | D# Eb

twelfth fret: E A D G B E

5

Various combinations or degrees of the 12 possible notes in the chromatic scale create other scales, which are normally seven specific notes. The note choice determines which scale you are playing. In the examples that follow, the chromatic scale begins with a selected pitch and is then numbered in sequence. Remember to memorize the number and associated letter of the note *and* where it is on the fretboard. Here's the chromatic scale and assigned numbers to the keys A and C. Sharps and flats are used to notate raised or lowered degrees in the chromatic scale.

Here's the chromatic scale, starting on A:

| Letter: | A | A# | B | C | C# | D | D# | E | F | F# | G | G# |
|---|---|---|---|---|---|---|---|---|---|---|---|---|
| Number: | 1 | #1 | 2 | b3 | 3 | 4 | #4 | 5 | #5 | 6 | b7 | 7 |

The A major scale is spelled: A, B, C#, D, E, F#, and G#.

| Letter: | **A** | A# | **B** | C | **C#** | **D** | D# | **E** | F | **F#** | G | **G#** |
|---|---|---|---|---|---|---|---|---|---|---|---|---|
| Number: | **1** | #1 | **2** | b3 | **3** | **4** | #4 | **5** | #5 | **6** | b7 | **7** |

And here's the chromatic scale, starting on C:

| Letter: | C | C# | D | Eb | E | F | D# | G | G# | A | Bb | B |
|---|---|---|---|---|---|---|---|---|---|---|---|---|
| Number: | 1 | #1 | 2 | b3 | 3 | 4 | #4 | 5 | #5 | 6 | b7 | 7 |

The C major scale is spelled: C, D, E, F, G, A, and B.

| Letter: | **C** | C# | **D** | Eb | **E** | **F** | D# | **G** | G# | **A** | Bb | **B** |
|---|---|---|---|---|---|---|---|---|---|---|---|---|
| Number: | **1** | #1 | **2** | b3 | **3** | **4** | #4 | **5** | #5 | **6** | b7 | **7** |

Make sure to know this in the common keys you play in—even better, in all 12 keys!

# Intervals ▶

**Intervals** are defined as the difference in pitch between two notes. The greater the difference in pitch, the larger the interval. As guitar players, we tend to think more in the difference in frets between two notes that are played. Intervals are the building blocks to music, and knowledge of this is very important to understand as it is the basis for grasping harmonies and melodies played on the guitar. Below is the chromatic scale we covered and the intervals used in all music. We will use the key of C in this example. (You will see this later in the book when we get to double stops.)

**Example 5**

**Example 6** `2:09`

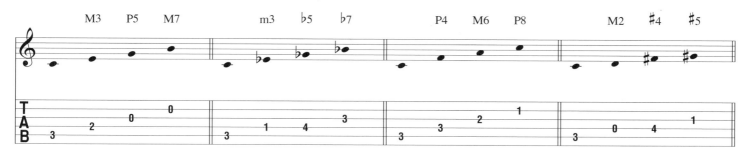

Note that the 2nd, 3rd, 6th, and 7th degrees are notated as major or minor, and intervals for 4ths and 5ths are either perfect, sharp, or flat, depending on the intervallic relationship. Intervals that share the notation like #4/♭5 are **enharmonic equivalents**, or equal to one another.

# Nashville Number System ▶

The vast majority of Nashville musicians speak in their own kind of language when it comes to chord charts and chart notation. This way of communicating is called the **Nashville Number System**. Traced back to the early '60s, this system is a style of charting out chord changes that session musician Charlie McCoy noticed the Jordanaires using on recording sessions. The system basically substitutes letters with numbers for a chord chart. This is a shorthand way of writing out chord progressions and communicating between *all* session players in Nashville.

It can really save you time, and here's a great example. Let's say your preparing to record or perform a song that is normally in the key of A. You've written the chart out only to find the vocalist is more comfortable singing the song in the key of C. Instead of re-writing the chart or transcribing it in real time during a performance, in the Nashville Number System, you would only change one thing: the key. All numbers stay the same, as they have the same relationship to the key of the song. It saves time and a lot of math you potentially could have to do on the fly. You will need to know a little basic theory and which chords are in a diatonic key. (**Diatonic** simply means, "in the key of.") Here's how it works with some chart examples.

This example is in the key of C, so the C major scale is spelled: C, D, E, F, G, A, and B.

Chords in the key of C:

| Letter: | C | Dm | Em | F | G | Am | B° |
|---------|---|----|----|----|----|----|----|
| Number: | 1 | 2m | 3m | 4 | 5 | 6m | 7° |

Each number is a degree of the scale, and each degree has a chord quality associated with it. The quality never changes if you stay in the key. This makes it easy to transpose very rapidly by assigning numbers instead of letters to the key.

Here's a chord chart example with some standard progressions. The first example is a standard letter chart, and the next is a Nashville Number System chart. Pay close attention to the chords and numbers assigned to each chord.

© 

$$\frac{4}{4}$$ ‖: 

| C | C | F | F |
| G | G | C | G |
| Am | F | G | C |
| Dm | Em | F | G :‖ |

© 

$$\frac{4}{4}$$ ‖: 

| 1 | 1 | 4 | 4 |
| 5 | 5 | 1 | 5 |
| 6m | 4 | 5 | 1 |
| 2m | 3m | 4 | 5 :‖ |

The second example is a little more complicated by adding **split bars**, or bars with more than one chord in them. Also included are **inversions,** or chords that don't contain the root in the bass. These chords may also be called **slash chords**. The way to notate these chords are to put the chord on top, then a slash (/), and then the note in the bass. In the example below, E/G# is an E chord with the G# in the bass and notated "1/3" in the number system. This occurs when walking up or down in the bass. This example also contains a (-) when notating minor chords. You can use the style of notating minor chords by using an (m) after the chord or a (-). Based on the preference of the chart writer, small variations of writing chords and other concepts may be slightly different in notation, but they all function the same.

Here's a minor chord example in key of E (F#m can be notated as 2m or 2-; the function and chord quality is the same.):

Ⓔ

| $\frac{4}{4}$ ‖: | E | A | (A B) | E |
|---|---|---|---|---|
| | E | A | (F#m $\frac{E}{G\sharp}$ A B) | E |
| | C#m | G#7 | A | E |
| | C#m | G#7 | (A $\frac{B}{D\sharp}$) | E :‖ |

Ⓔ

| $\frac{4}{4}$ ‖: | 1 | 4 | (4 5) | 1 |
|---|---|---|---|---|
| | 1 | 4 | (2- $\frac{1}{3}$ 4 5) | 1 |
| | 6- | $3^7$ | 4 | 1 |
| | 6- | $3^7$ | (4 $\frac{5}{7}$) | 1 :‖ |

# Scales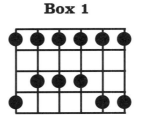

## Pentatonic Scales/Patterns

This section of the book heavily utilizes a scale you're probably already familiar with: the **pentatonic scale**. It's made up of five notes and can be used over most chords and progressions. Here are the basic box patterns that we'll explore in major and minor tonalities.

**Box 1**

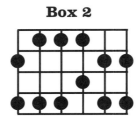

**Box 2**

**Box 3**

**Box 4**

**Box 5**

# Major Pentatonic Licks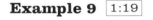

Here are some licks that exclusively use the notes in the major pentatonic scale. Remember that the major pentatonic is spelled: 1, 2, 3, 5, and 6. Note that there are slide articulations in each lick, allowing you to shift up and down the neck. As you progress in this book, there will be many kinds of articulations or embellishments by adding various techniques to finesse the harmonic line. This gives you a more lyrical quality and makes your playing "sing" more. Pay close attention to the fingerings as well. Economy of motion is crucial, and it's made possible by playing the correct fingering. This allows you to play faster with little wasted effort.

**Example 7**

**Example 8**　0:40

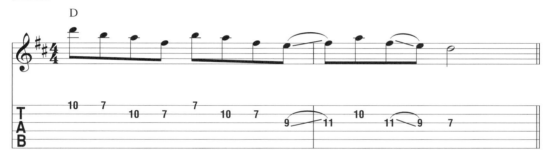

**Example 9**　1:19

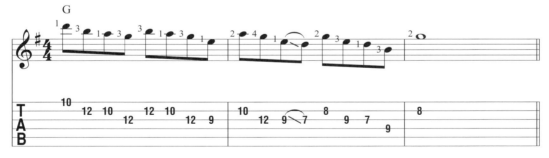

**Example 10**　2:04

11

# Minor Pentatonic Licks

Minor is another tonality and is relative to major. The relative minor to major can always be found by descending a minor 3rd or three frets on the guitar neck from the major. For example, in the key of G, go down three frets and the relative minor would be Em or the 6m (6-) in numbers. Think of major as "happy" and minor as "sad" when it comes to chords and the emotions they evoke. Understanding the quality of chords helps you decide what to play over that chord. The minor pentatonic scale can be spelled in intervals as: 1, ♭3, 4, 5, and ♭7.

As you begin to get more comfortable with ascending and descending scales in a box form, start to move up and down the neck with embellishments like hammer-ons/pull-offs and slides, which should be struck once and played with the left hand playing a higher or lower note without picking. Skip notes in the scale to add more flavor and color. Here are a few examples in several different keys.

**Example 11**

**Example 12** `1:08`

**Example 13** `1:48`

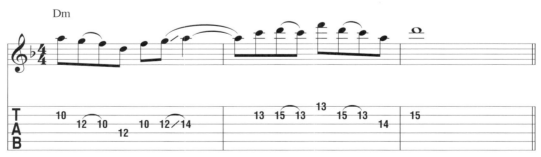

**Example 14** `2:18`

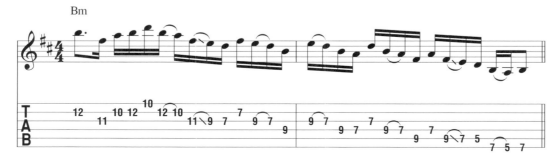

12

# Country Composite Scale ▶

The **country composite scale** is a six-note scale that adds a flatted 3rd (♭3) to the major pentatonic scale. This extra note adds a little chromaticism to the scale, as it has three consecutive notes in it. The extra flavor or color sounds very "country" and is also used in bluegrass music. Below are examples that use the box shape for this scale. Make sure to map out the entire neck with the specific notes in this scale and be able to move freely through all the positions on the neck.

The formula for this scale is spelled: 1, 2, ♭3, 3, 5, and 6. For the first four examples, we will use the A Country Composite scale and go up the entire neck. The notes used will be A, B, C, C♯, E, and F♯. The final two examples will use the E Country Composite scale, which is spelled: E, F♯, G, G♯, B, and C♯. Pay close attention to the phrasing and fingerings for each lick.

**Example 15**

**Example 16**  1:25

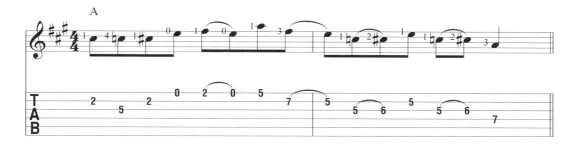

**Example 17**  2:42

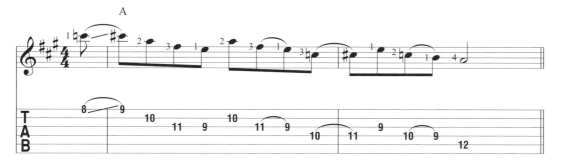

**Example 18**  3:53

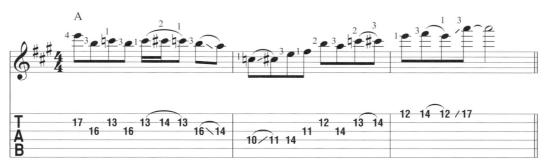

**Example 19** `4:24`

**Example 20** `5:27`

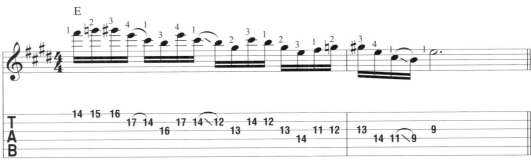

# Blues Scale

The **blues scale** is essentially a minor pentatonic scale with an added blue note (♭5) and is spelled: 1, ♭3, 4, ♭5, 5, and ♭7. Three chromatic notes in a row add nice color, and the ♭3, ♭5, and ♭7 intervals work great for country music. This scale works very well and adds flavor and built-in chromaticism to your note choices.

Below are examples using only single-note lines and are great licks to play over chords. Blues playing tends to use a lot of bends, but for these examples, we will stay with the articulations of hammer-ons, pull-offs, and slides for now. (Later in the book, we will add bends and other embellishments.) Also included in the examples are licks in keys that some guitar players tend to shy away from: flat keys. **Tip:** It's always good to practice in all 12 keys to be more prepared. If you find a lick you like, you can always move it to any key by using the information shown in the Interval section in this book.

**Example 21**

**Example 22** `3:44`

**Example 23**  `5:19`

**Example 24**  `5:42`

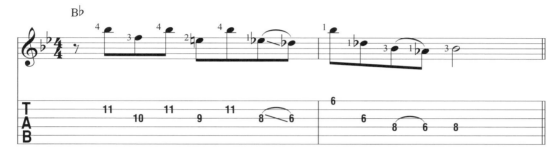

**Example 25**  `6:22`

# Bluegrass Scale (Mixolydian add♭3) ▶

The **bluegrass scale** is a departure from the standard Mixolydian scale, which is the fifth mode in a major key. This altered scale is spelled: 1, 2, ♭3, 3, 4, 5, 6, and ♭7. The addition of a ♭3 makes it an altered scale with eight total notes. This selection of notes is used very often in bluegrass and has four chromatic notes in a row. With this scale, you are playing two thirds of all possible notes, and chromaticism is built right into the scale. There are lots of colors to paint with in this scale. For the following examples, we will use the keys of G and D.

The G bluegrass scale is spelled: G, A, B♭, B, C, D, E, and F.

**Example 26**

15

**Example 27**  `1:49`

**Example 28**  `2:23`

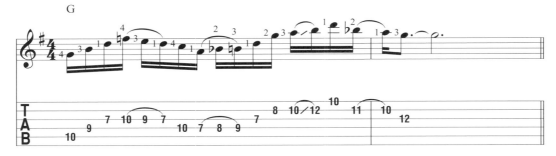

The D bluegrass scale is spelled: D, E, F, F♯, G, A, B, and C.

**Example 29**  `3:32`

**Example 30**  `4:23`

**Example 31**  `5:57`

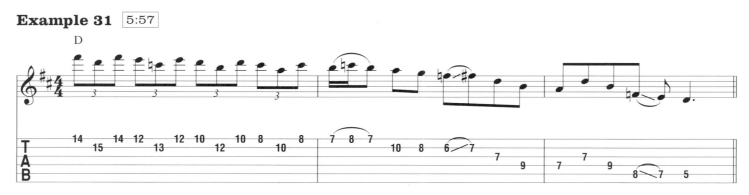

16

# The CAGED System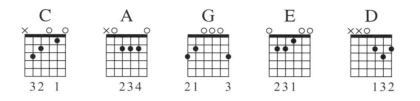

The **CAGED system** is a different way of visualizing the fretboard and playing over a chord or chord progression. Scales are a single-note way of playing over a chord, while the CAGED system is focused more on the chord and the shape of the voicings and multiple notes within that chord. It's a great way of mapping out the fretboard and visualizing the shape and notes within each chord. The CAGED system is five simple block voicings found commonly in open-position chords. For most of us, these are the first chords we learn as beginners, C–A–G–E–D, hence the name "CAGED" system. Below are the five open-voiced chords.

Here are some examples of using the CAGED system in open position. Play each corresponding chord before playing the lick examples. This will help you visualize the chord shapes and the notes selected. Examples in this section are either in ascending or descending form. Make sure to follow the left-hand fingerings and articulations (hammer-ons, pull-offs, and slides).

**Example 32**

**Example 33**  `3:34`

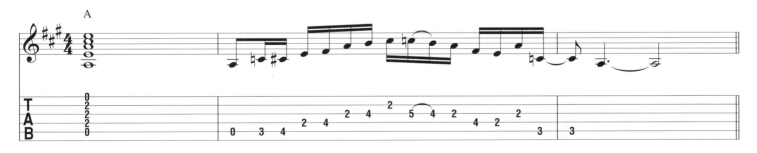

**Example 34**  `4:01`

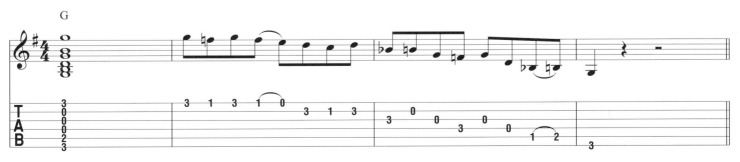

**Example 35** `4:34`

**Example 36** `4:59`

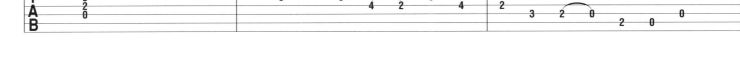

# CAGED Shapes Up the Neck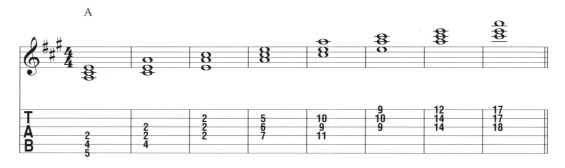

Now let's take the shape of these chords, move them up the neck, and play the chord in three-note clusters using the shapes in the CAGED system. Here are the block voicings for the key of A, using CAGED chord shapes. These block voicings can be great to use when comping or playing rhythm guitar. They can add character to a chord without harmonically getting in the way, as you are repeating the same notes, just in a different orientation.

**Example 37**

In this next example, you will play a triplet pattern and use the pick, middle finger, and ring finger on the right hand. For the descending pattern, simply reverse the right hand to ring finger, middle finger, and then the pick. An **arpeggio** (Italian word for "broken chord") is a great way of highlighting the chord by playing one note at a time. With each shape you will get slightly different sounding combinations as the shape changes. These inversions still outline the chord and are simply voiced or arranged in different intervallic patterns. This is essential to understand and visualize in order to play ascending or descending lines over a chord.

Here is an example of playing an arpeggio, ascending up the neck in the key of A. Note that we are using the same shape and blocked voicing, but just breaking up the chord, playing it one note at a time. Make sure to do this in every key and become more comfortable with the fingerings and position shifting. Here it is in ascending form:

**Example 38** `2:12`

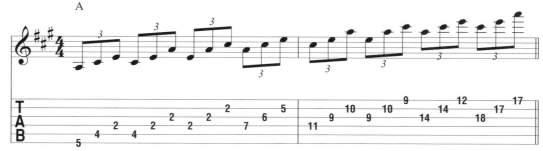

And descending form:

**Example 39** `2:40`

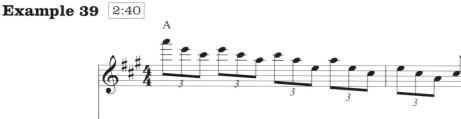

# Playing a Progression Using CAGED Positions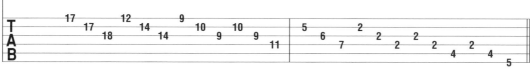

Now let's get to playing multiple chords in a row, using the CAGED system. These examples will cover a 1–4–5 progression for each key.

Example 40 is in G and uses the open position for the solo. Repeat the example to gain fluidity in the lines and connecting the notes over each chord.

**Example 40**

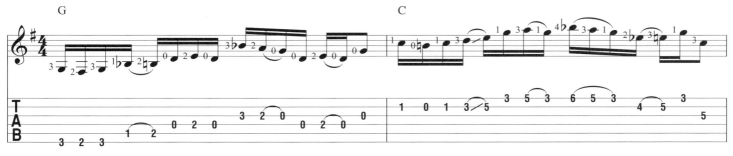

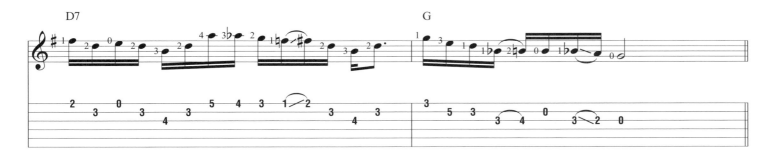

Example 41 is played in the moveable chord form of barre chords. Notice there is a repetitive line to start that uses open strings. This example in the key of C uses open-position and moveable chord forms for each chord. Note the fingerings and repeat the section.

**Example 41**  1:51

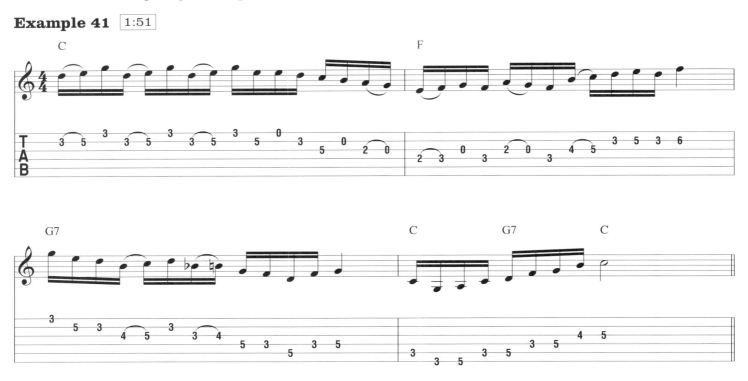

Example 42 is in the key of E, and it moves up the neck primarily from the fourth to seventh frets on the neck. Each note can be picked with exception to hammer-ons or pull-offs.

**Example 42**  2:36

The final example in the key of B uses multiple chord forms for each part of the progression. This gives you more access to notes found on different strings and positions on the neck. Notice there is a string-skipping part over the 5 chord (F#). Use the middle finger on the right hand to play the notes on the B string. Pay close attention to the left-hand fingerings, as they will allow you to play this example with no wasted movement and set you up to correctly execute the solo.

**Example 43** 3:28

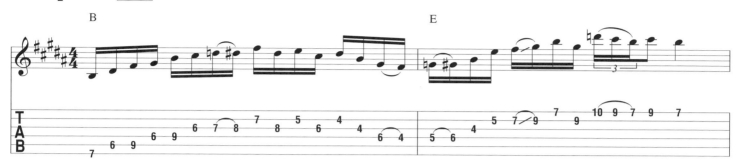

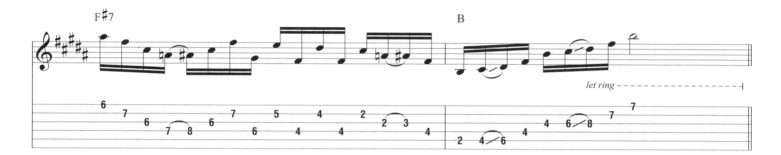

# Country Techniques

## Open-String Licks

**Open-string licks** are a great way of incorporating the non-fretted notes on the guitar into melodic lines that may not necessarily be in open position. Playing open-string runs can create great tension and release and really can add to a country guitar player's bag of tricks. You have five options for open notes (E, A, D, G, and B), so the possible combinations need to contain those notes. (Certain keys work better than others.) Remember when playing these licks to let the open notes and single notes played on consecutive strings to ring into each other, as this creates a nice cascading effect to the line that you're playing. As always, use hybrid picking throughout each example.

Let's start with using the open strings in the G major scale.

**Example 44**

Now try C major:

**Example 45** `1:44`

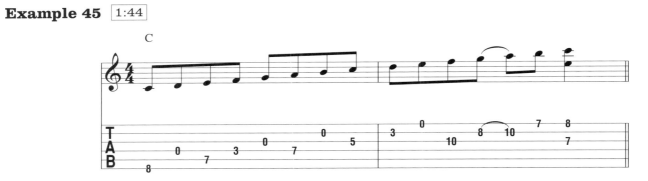

Next, try E major:

**Example 46** `3:12`

Here are several open-string examples with ascending and descending lines over a single chord.

**Example 47**  4:13

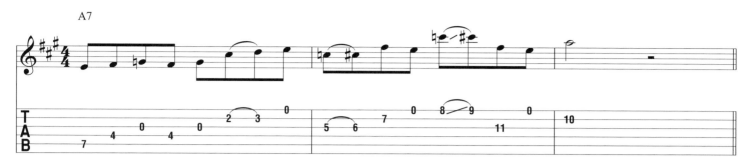

**Example 48**  4:40

**Example 49**  5:12

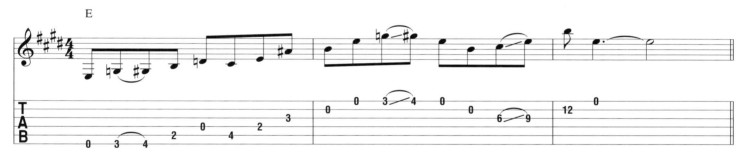

**Example 50**  5:38

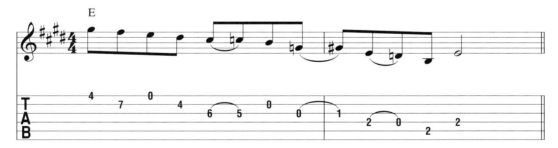

**Example 51**  6:20

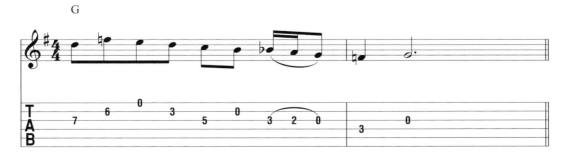

**Example 52** 6:42

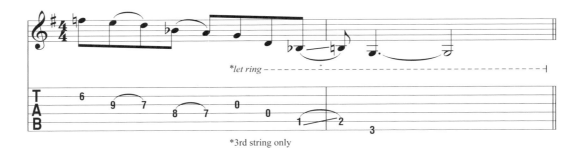

*let ring -------------- - - - - - - - - - - - - - - - - - -*

*3rd string only

**Example 53** 7:05

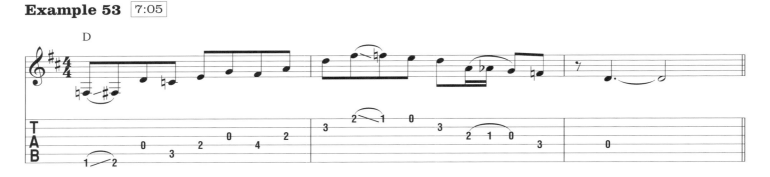

**Example 54** 7:31

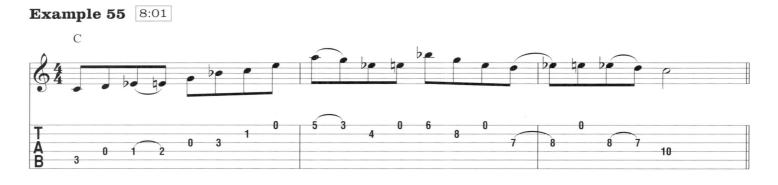

**Example 55** 8:01

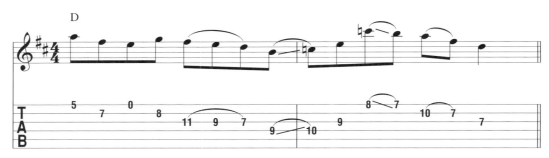

**Example 56** 8:29

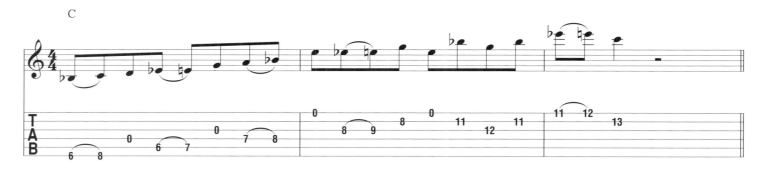

24

You can also play open-string licks over minor chords. Here are a few examples.

**Example 57** `8:58`

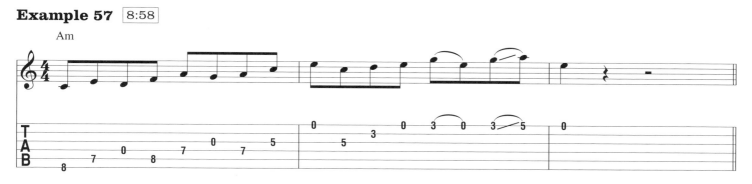

**Example 58** `9:39`

**Example 59** `10:08`

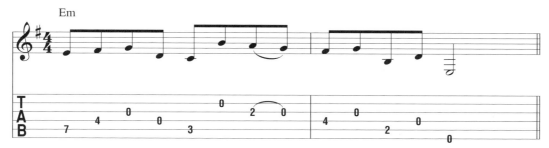

You can also use several open-string licks together to play over a progression. This example works over a 1–4–5 progression in A. Notice that this is a repetitive sequence that outlines the chords.

**Example 60** `11:17`

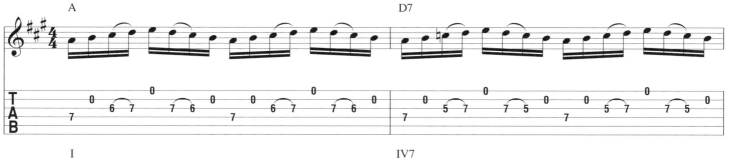

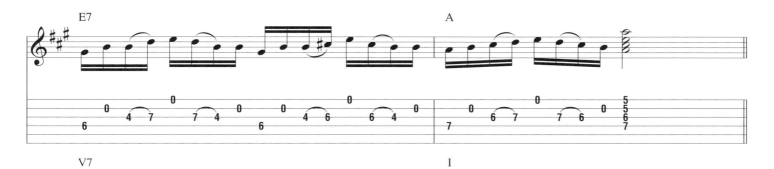

And here's an example in E:

**Example 61**  `13:25`

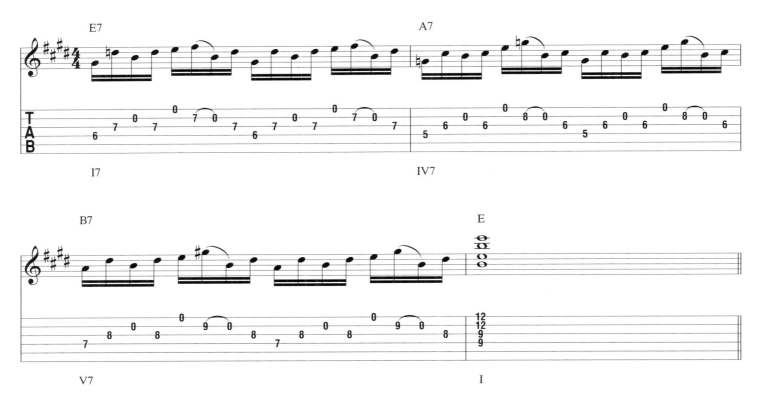

# Double Stops ▶

**Double stops** are two notes played simultaneously and are a very important technique used by country guitar players. The term comes from the violin technique of playing two strings at once. For guitar, the "stop" is a common technique of cutting off the double note and making the attack quick or slightly muted. This is achieved in two ways. You can cut the note off with the pick and middle finger on the right hand, or use the palm of the right hand to dampen the attack of the note. You may also let double notes ring out, depending on the application of this technique. The difference between the two notes played is defined by their interval. Double stops may be played on adjacent strings or by skipping strings, depending on the size of the interval. Common intervals used are 3rds, 4ths, tritones, 5ths, and 6ths, but any interval is fair game in this technique. In this technique, you will need some right-hand independence. The pick plays one note while the middle finger will usually strike the second note on the string below.

Here are some examples of harmonizing the major scale with double stops of varying intervals. Remember to work on varying the note length of each double stop. For each example, use the pick and the right-hand middle finger to strike the two notes.

**Example 62**

**Example 63** `1:50`

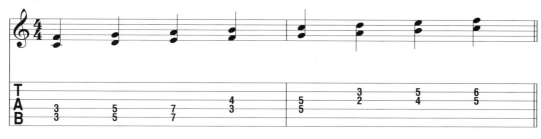

**Example 64** `2:16`

**Example 65** `2:49`

Now let's begin using the double-stop technique in licks over a chord. In the following examples, we will be using several possible intervals. It is important to know which interval you're playing. Interval recognition is crucial in constructing and understanding what is going on in the following licks. Double stops can really fatten up your lines, making it sound like two guitar players are playing at once. Single notes will be used to connect the double stops over these licks. You will be using slides, hammer-ons, and pull-offs as articulations in connecting the note choices.

**Example 66** `3:35`

**Example 67** `4:07`

**Example 68**  5:08

**Example 69**  7:03

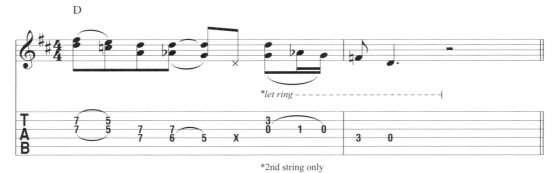

*let ring ---------------------------|

*2nd string only

**Example 70**  8:00

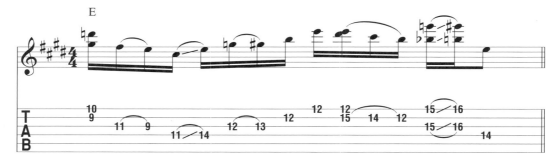

**Example 71**  8:24

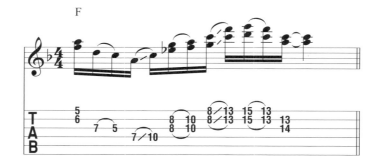

28

**Example 72** 9:28

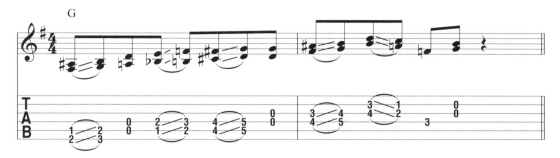

Here are a few examples using double stops and open strings.

**Example 73** 10:40

**Example 74** 11:12

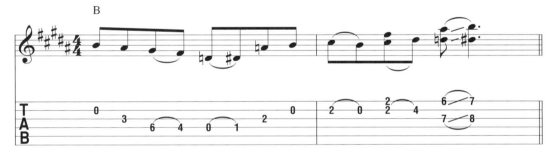

You can even use this technique over minor chords.

**Example 75** 12:45

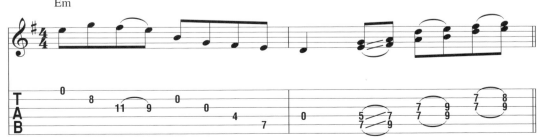

**Example 76** 14:15

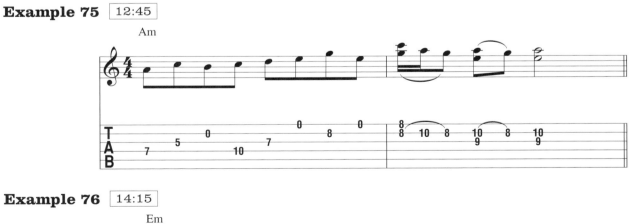

## Playing Double Stops Through Chord Changes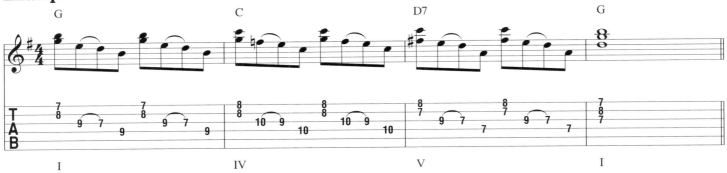

Here are some examples playing through chord changes, using repetitive sequences and double stops. The changes are 1, 4, and 5 chords in the keys of the G, C, and E.

**Example 77**

# Bending Strings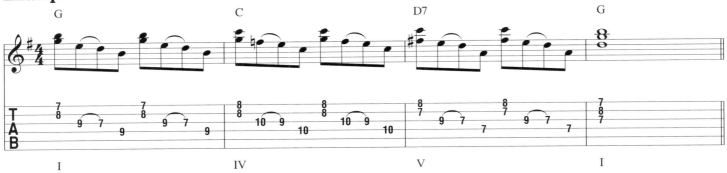

String bending in country guitar playing is approached differently than blues and rock bending in several ways. A common difference is **oblique motion**, which is the technique of playing other notes against a held-note bend. Another departure is the use of the middle and index fingers on the left hand when bending notes, which is not so commonly used in other styles of music. You may bend notes from a quarter step up to a step and a half. The most common bends are either full steps or half steps. Many licks may also be derived from mimicking the sound and phrasing of the pedal steel guitar. We will cover many different ways to approach this very unique and sometimes difficult way of playing this technique. You will need to really use your ear-training and make sure you are accurate so that the notes are properly intonated (in tune). It may take some time to develop the muscles and correct technique to achieve some of these bends. Through proper practice and patience, you'll be adding a very powerful and useful tool to your bag country of licks and tricks.

The first two examples are simple unison full-step bends on the G and B strings up the neck. In these two examples, you will use your ring finger to bend and your index finger to play the other note (unless it is on an open string). Listen closely to when the note is in tune after bending. Creating tension in the bent notes is fine, but you want to strive for an exactly matching pitch between the two notes.

**Example 80**

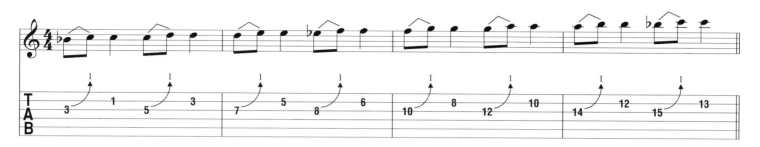

**Example 81**  `3:12`

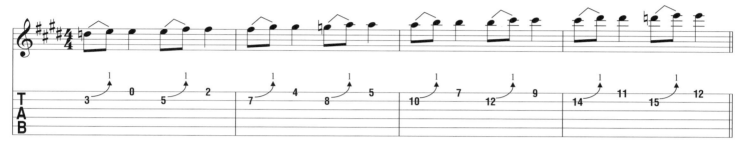

# Oblique Motion Bends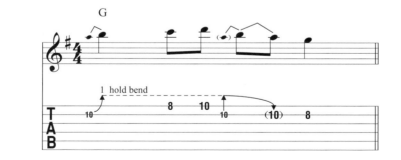

Here are some examples of oblique-motion bends, starting simple and moving to more difficult. Notice that you must hold the bent note and play other single notes while doing this. The note choices can create wonderful tension. Once the bent note is released, an eventual resolve is brought to the phrase. This is a quintessential part of music: tension and release. Here are some examples of oblique bends and licks. Pay close attention to the fingerings and how long notes are bent and then released.

**Example 82**

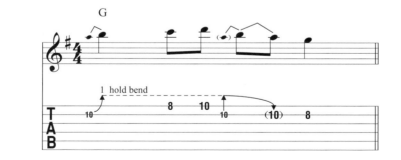

**Example 83**  `1:16`

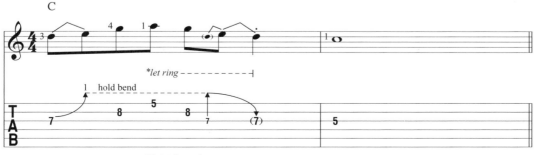

*1st string only

31

**Example 84** `1:42`

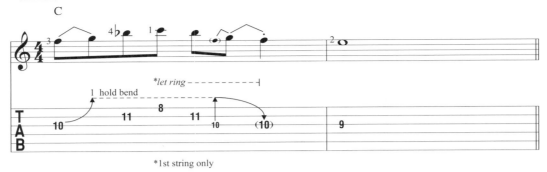

*1st string only

**Example 85** `2:47`

**Example 86** `4:15`

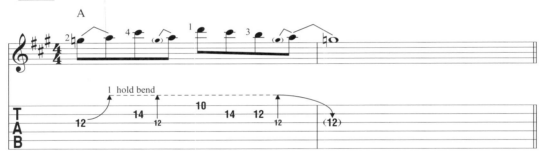

# Chicken Pickin' and Bending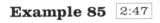

Another technique you can add is a rhythmic "cluck" used in **chicken picking**. The cluck is written as an (x), or dead note. The rhythmic placement is important to get as it sets up the phrasing of the lick. Here are several examples moving up the neck over a chord, using the "cluck" technique and bends. Take notice that some examples use half-step bends and the technique of **pre-bending**, or bending the note prior to picking and then releasing it. An important thing to remember is to allow the top, unbent note to ring while bending and releasing the note below. (Of course, this is just an option.)

**Example 87**

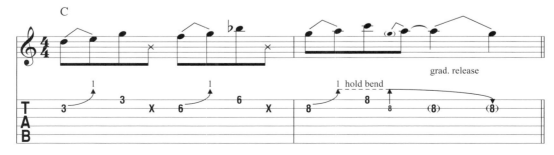

**Example 88**  `1:09`

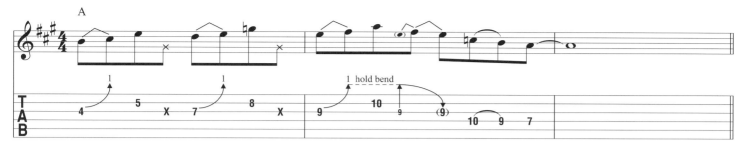

**Example 89**  `2:16`

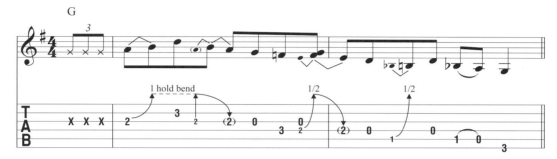

**Example 90**  `3:33`

# Multiple Bends Within a Phrase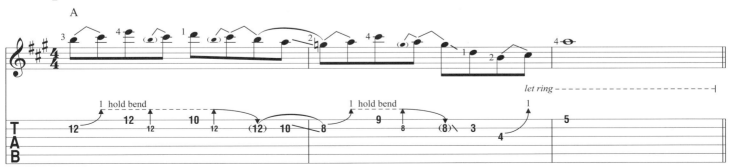

Now let's add multiple bends to create more complex lines. In the following examples, you will be bending more than once and on different strings. There are many combinations you can create to flavor your licks with bends.

**Example 91**

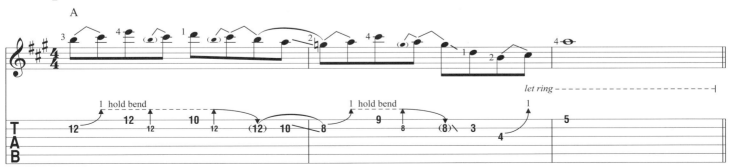

**Example 92**  `1:15`

**Example 93**  `2:11`

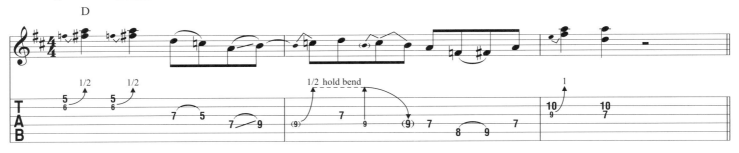

**Example 94**  `3:27`

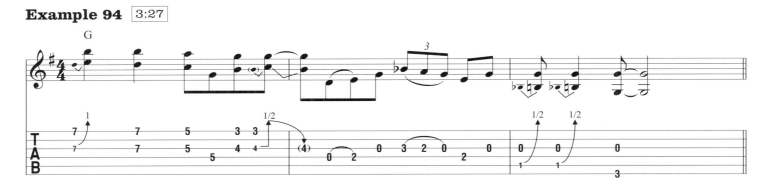

**Example 95**  `4:53`

# Pedal Steel Bends

**Pedal steel bends** can give the guitar a very unique sound by emulating the tone and phrasing of a pedal steel guitar. The pedal steel guitar achieves the bends through the use of knee and foot levers that bend the pitch by half or whole steps, either up or down. With some specialized modifications, bends of even more than a whole step can be achieved. This gives you several possibilities of expression for note choices and how to manipulate the desired pitch. Combined with the fact there are multiple tuning options, you can see the possibilities are endless for note choices and ways to manipulate them.

Following are some basic examples of licks in the style of pedal steel guitar. (Remember to hold the top, unbent note of each bending figure.)

**Example 96**

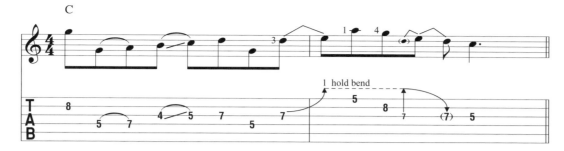

**Example 97** `2:35`

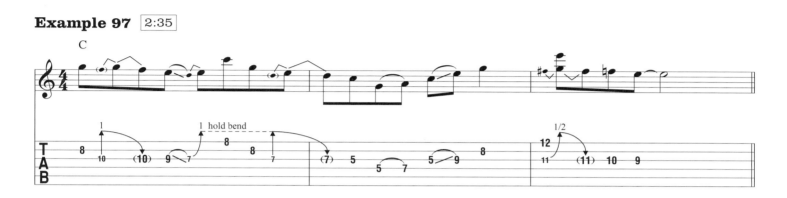

**Example 98** `4:24`

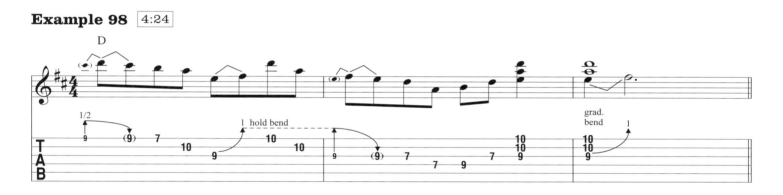

**Example 99** `5:51`

**Example 100** `7:52`

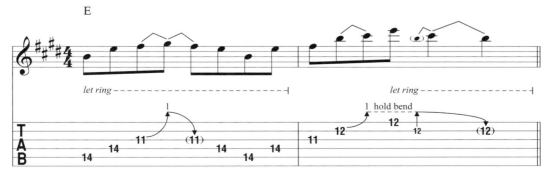

# Bending in Uncommon Keys

Here are some examples in keys that may be not so common for guitar players.

**Example 101**

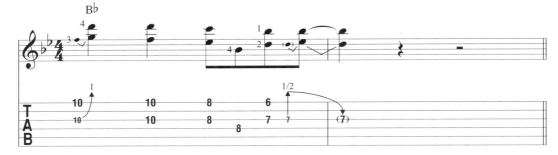

**Example 102** `2:03`

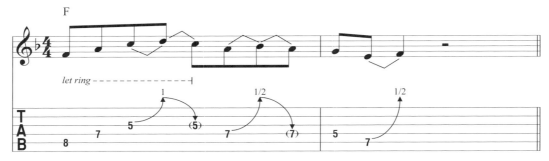

**Example 103** `4:02`

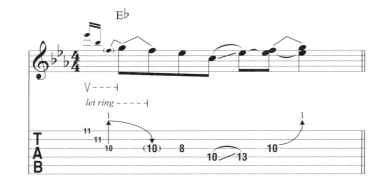

**Example 104** `5:33`

# Putting the Pieces Together ▶

We've covered several techniques in this book with a focus on single-note lines, double stops, open-string licks, and bends and how they are used in country music. The licks and lines shown to you are but fragments of what constitutes this music. Licks are typically great for playing over one or two chords. However, when you start playing over a progression or several chords and in longer durations, you need to bring your ideas together to make a cohesive musical thought. Phrases, the use of space, note choices, and correct rhythm playing to create tension and release is the ultimate goal when crafting a solo.

We are now going to move our focus to making music and not just playing licks over static chords. What I've provided in the next seven solo examples are different approaches to creating phrases and lines over several common feels and progressions found in country music.

## Solo 1: Train Beat in A ▶

We start off with a simple, eight-bar progression over a very common feel of a **train beat** in the key of A. This eight-bar solo is designed to be played twice (repeated). Using single-note lines to connect bends and then a quick double-stop, this can be considered an entry level solo. It is an easy yet effective way of playing over a very common progression in country music (1–4–5). This solo also stays in the lower register of the neck, so you won't have to concentrate on shifting positions. The main focus is to connect the lines and play the phrases rhythmically correct.

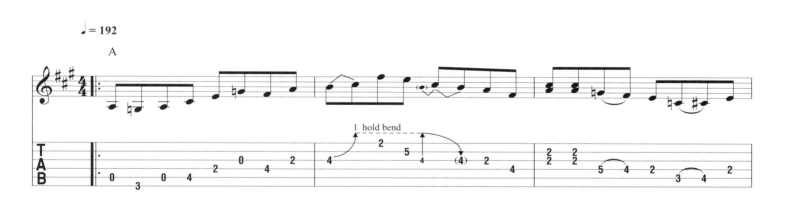

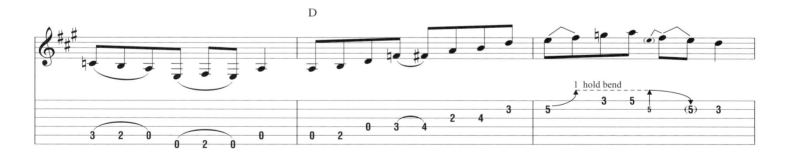

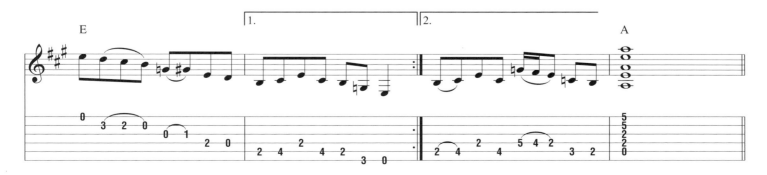

# Solo 2: Train Beat in G

This solo is a variation from Solo 1 and in a different key. We'll use the same train-beat feel, but much more is going on regarding techniques used and note choices. This eight-bar progression is played twice. We will now be connecting all four techniques (single-note lines, double stops, pedal steel bends, and open strings) we have worked on to create phrases over the chord progression. Pay close attention to the articulations with hammer-ons, pull-offs, and slides that move up and down the neck. Positioning and fingerings are crucial to executing the phrases properly. Start slow and work on the solo a bar or two at a time to build up consistency throughout the piece.

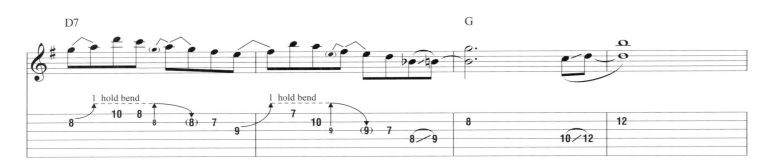

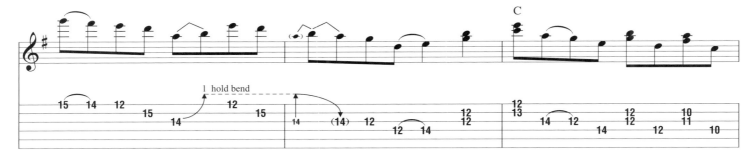

# Solo 3: Two-Beat Feel in C

This solo contains several new concepts as well as another common feel for country, the **two-beat** (two beats per measure). This progression also has a minor tonality but is still in the key of C. In country music, keys are always in major and never minor. The main focus on this piece is phrasing over the bar, using mostly double stops. The use of the neck or middle pickup on the guitar is recommended for a smoother tone. Rhythm and timing are essential to play this soulful solo with lots of position shifting.

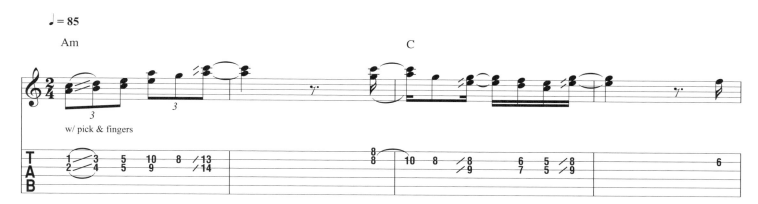

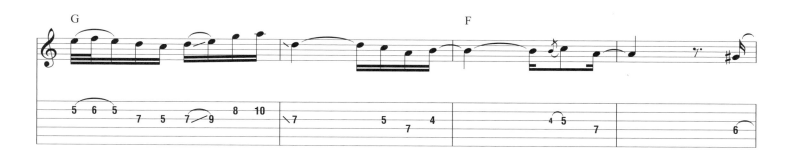

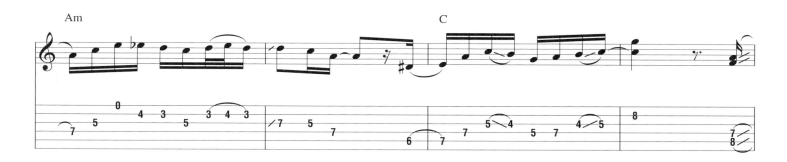

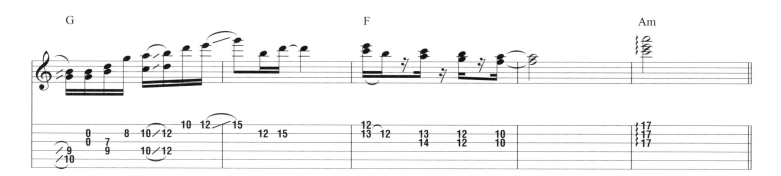

# Solo 4: Shuffle Feel in E ▶

This solo is played over a shuffle feel and goes outside the usual diatonic chord structure, using the 2 chord as a major chord (it would be minor otherwise). This allows us to play outside the key and harmonically opens up more possibilities. This solo contains more tension using chromaticism to connect chords and uses half-step slides into double stops. Chicken picking and use of dead notes adds a rhythmic flare to this piece. This is a great example of approaching chords from a half step below to create tension through chromaticism. Fingering and phrasing are also important to getting this solo correct.

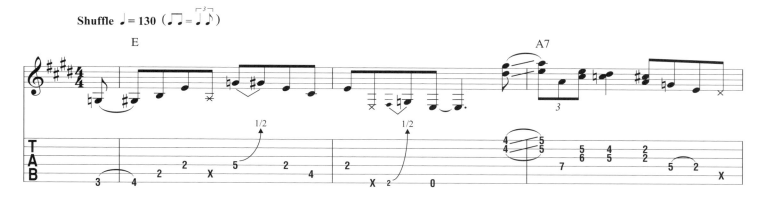

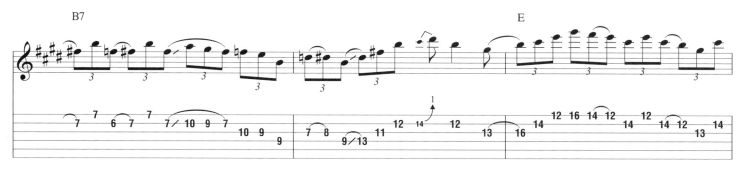

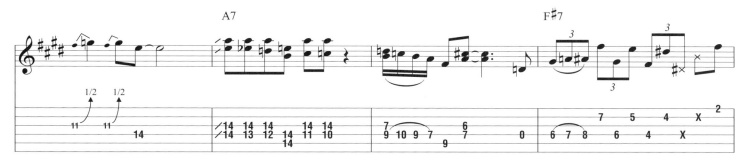

# Solo 5: Four-on-the-Floor in A

This feel, made famous by outlaw writers like Waylon Jennings, has a great driving beat with the kick drum on every quarter note, hence the term **four-on-the-floor**. A sequential, double-stop rhythm is used over the first two times through this progression of 1–♭7–4–1. The third pass uses an open-string idea shown to you earlier in the book and expands to fit the chord changes. The fourth and final pass contains a pedal-tone idea with a string-skipping technique to round out the ideas used in this solo. Very rhythmic and driving, this solo uses some great ideas to play when adding a ♭7 chord (G) in the key of A.

♩ = 120

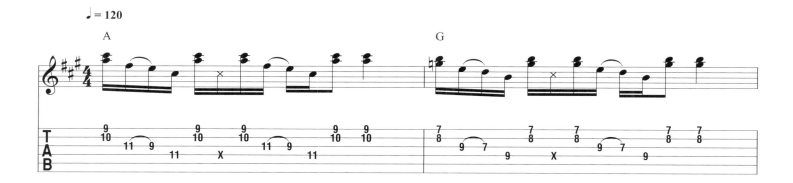

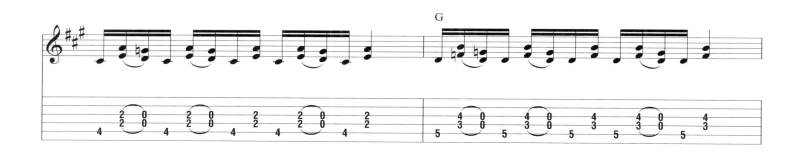

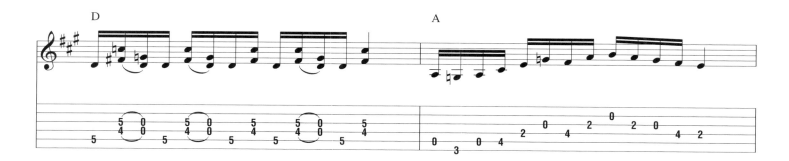

42

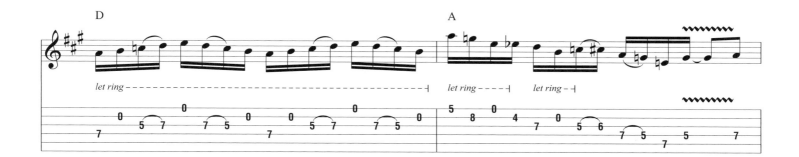

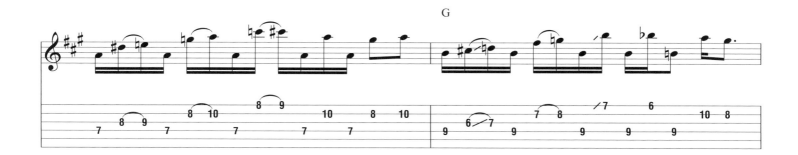

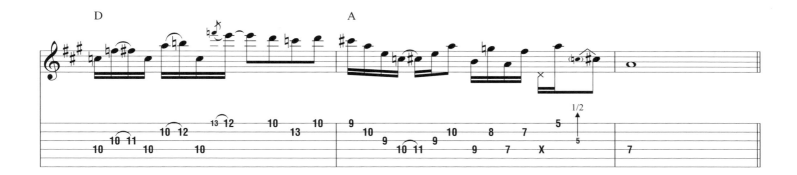

# Solo 6: Swing Feel in B♭ ▶

In this example, we really stretch out some of the harmonic possibilities over a standard turnaround of 1–6–2m–5 in the not-so-guitar-friendly key of B♭. When you play jazz or western swing, you will see songs in flat keys. It is a great way to work on playing in a key that you might not be so comfortable in. In this lazy swing feel, I've included lots of altered notes and borrowed from the **harmonic** and **melodic minor scales**, specifically over the 2m and 5 chords. The 5 chord (F) is altered to an **augmented chord**, which lends itself to using those scales. As we really haven't covered harmonic and melodic minor scales, just be aware of which chord tone you are playing against the chord. It may sound a little different, but that's the point—creating tension to then release it. There are several triplet rhythms in this solo as well. I recommend to play this example on the neck pickup for a warmer tone.

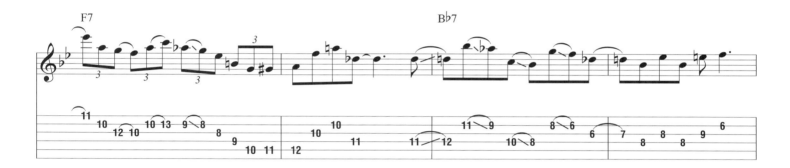

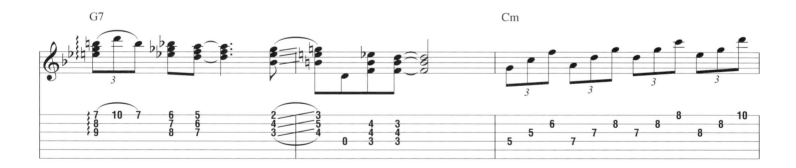

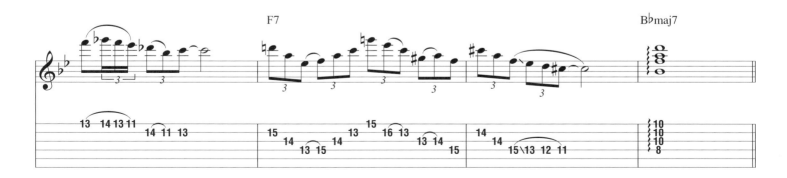

# Solo 7: Fast Train Beat in D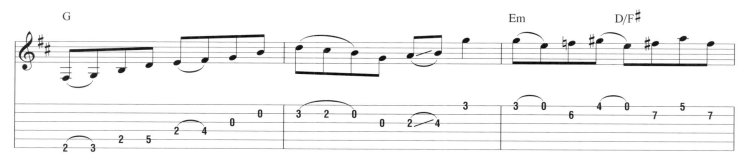

In the final installment of country solos, we showcase all the ideas we have worked on in this book over a fast train beat in the key of D. Included in the chord changes are split bars, or bars with more than one chord. The 2m–1/3–4–5 is found very often in country music and is a great way of creating movement in your chord changes. There is a fair amount of chromaticism in **passing tones** to connect chords, and this piece highlights the possibilities of choices when traversing the entire neck. Start with playing smaller phrases of one, two, or four bars, and work your way through both solos. Chicken picking, as well as rakes in the right hand, are important techniques that add character to the phrases. Articulations and correct left-hand fingerings are a must in order to switch between all the techniques used and positioning on the neck.

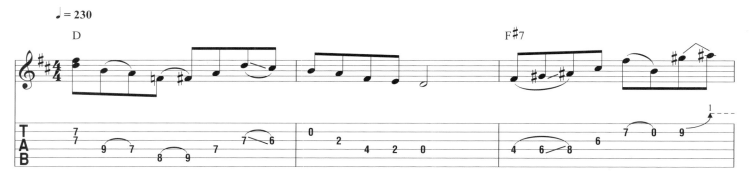

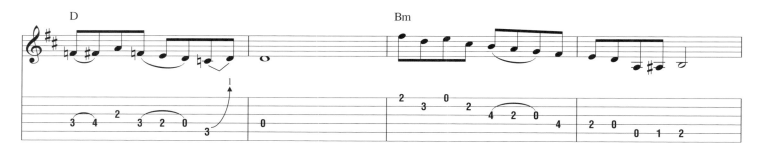

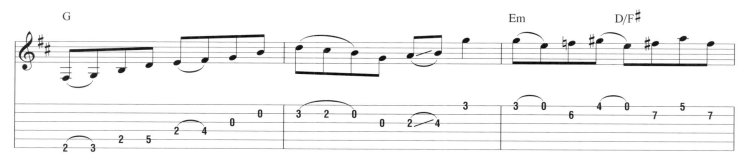

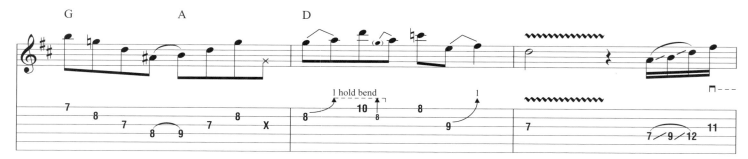

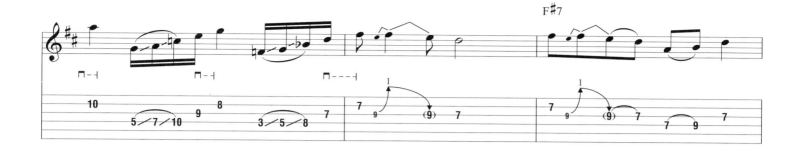

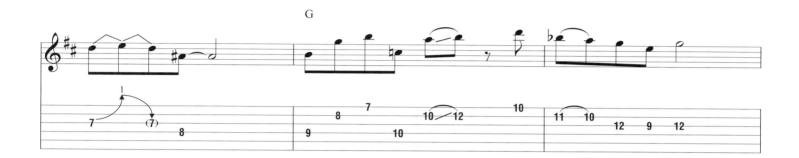

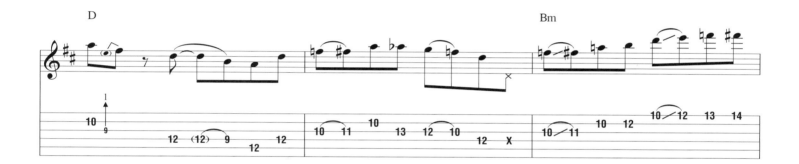

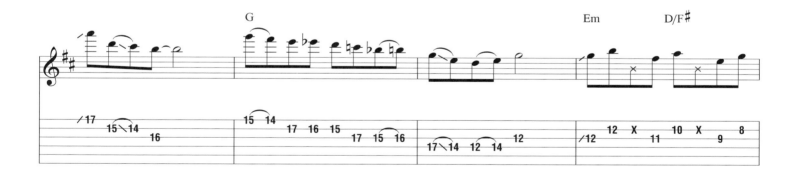

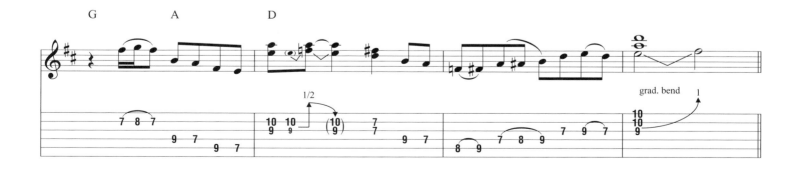

# Recommended Guitar Players

Here's a list of recommended guitar players to inspire you in your journey of learning country guitar techniques. Some names you may recognize, others may be new to you. By no means is this a list of every great guitar player out there, but it's a good representation of the talent on country guitar. I encourage you to check out each person's playing style and music. Each one has their own unique approach and voice to playing country guitar. The list is in no particular order.

| | | |
|---|---|---|
| Redd Volkaert | Brent Mason | Pat Bergeson |
| Danny Gatton | Eugene Moles | Pat Buchanan |
| Jerry Reed | James Mitchell | Danny Muhammad |
| Leon Rhodes | Jerry Donahue | Tom Bukovac |
| Grady Martin | Will Ray | Andy Wood |
| Scotty Anderson | John Jorgenson | Chris Scruggs |
| Merle Travis | Ray Flacke | Rory Hoffman |
| Chet Atkins | Pete Anderson | Rod Riley |
| Brad Paisley | Clarence White | Johnny Hiland |
| Jimmy Bryant | James Burton | Craig Smith |
| Junior Brown | Steve Wariner | Chuck Ward |
| Roy Nichols | Jimmy Capps | Guthrie Trapp |
| Don Rich | Jim Campilongo | Landon Jordon |
| Vince Gill | Kenny Vaughn | Jim Oblon |
| Albert Lee | Jimmy Montiac | Mike Borque |
| Reggie Young | Tony Rice | Kevin Ray |
| Hank Garland | Doc Watson | John 5 |
| Jimmy Orlander | Scott Fore | |
| Clint Strong | Marty Stuart | |

# About the Author

Matthew Lee has been playing guitar professionally for over 25 years and has been a Nashville native for the last 12 years. He has two music degrees from the University of Wisconsin-Oshkosh in Music Recording and Business. He has toured the United States and Europe extensively and has been a band leader and member for such acts as Shooter Jennings, Jessi Colter, Doug Stone, and Ray Scott. His playing has been featured on the Grand Ole Opry and several network television shows as a guitar sideman. In addition, he has logged thousands of gigs in the local Nashville scene in honky-tonks and live music venues, playing endless sets of country music. He is the co-founder of Nashville Guitar Community, a guitar-based online community that hosts local events featuring guitar players. For more information on Matthew, including his music and much more, go to *www.matthewleeguitar.com*.